10/9 5

United States v. Nixon (1974)

By MARK E. DUDLEY

TWENTY-FIRST CENTURY
BOOKS
A Division of
Henry Holt and Company

New York

To the memory of A. H.

Twenty-First Century Books
A Division of Henry Holt and Company, Inc.
115 West 18th Street
New York, NY 10011

Henry Holt® and colophon are trademarks of
Henry Holt and Company, Inc.
Publishers since 1866

Published in Canada by Fitzhenry & Whiteside Ltd.,
195 Allstate Parkway, Markham, Ontario, L3R 4T8

Library of Congress Cataloging-in-Publication Data
Dudley, Mark E.
United States v. Nixon (1974) : presidential powers / Mark E. Dudley. — 1st ed.
p. cm. — (Supreme Court decisions)
Includes bibliographical references and index.
  1. United States—Trials, litigation, etc.—Juvenile literature. 2. Nixon, Richard M. (Richard Milhous), 1913-1994
—Trials, litigation, etc.—Juvenile literature. 3. Executive privilege (Government information)—United States—
Juvenile literature. 4. Watergate Affair, 1972-1974—Juvenile literature.
[1. Watergate Affair, 1972-1974. 2. Nixon, Richard M. (Richard Milhous), 1913-1994—Trials, litigation, etc.]
I. Title. II. Series: Supreme Court decisions (New York, N.Y.)
KF228.U5D83 1994b   342.73'06— dc20   94-21863
[347.3026]   CIP AC

Photo Credits
All photos provided by AP / Wide World Photos.

Design
Tina Tarr-Emmons

Typesetting and Layout
Custom Communications

ISBN 0-8050-3658-X
First Edition 1994

Printed in Mexico
All first editions are printed on acid-free paper ∞.
10 9 8 7 6 5 4 3 2 1

Contents

Cast of Characters. **iv**

Timeline of Events. **vii**

Introduction

    "I Have Impeached Myself" **9**

Chapter One

    Watergate Break-in **11**

Chapter Two

    Cover-up **19**

Chapter Three

    Cover-up Exposed **29**

Chapter Four

    Battle for the Tapes **39**

Chapter Five

    Saturday Night Massacre **49**

Chapter Six

    Presidential Powers **59**

Chapter Seven

    The Court Decides **75**

Chapter Eight

    Aftermath **85**

    Source Notes **88**

    Further Reading **93**

    Index **95**

Cast of Characters

Spiro Agnew	39th Vice President of the United States
Bernard Baker	One of the Watergate burglars
Senator Howard Baker	Member of the Senate Watergate Committee
Carl Bernstein	*Washington Post* reporter who, with Bob Woodward, first wrote about Watergate scandal
Alexander Butterfield	Deputy assistant to H. R. Haldeman
Charles Colson	Special counsel to President Nixon
Archibald Cox	First Watergate Special Prosecutor
John W. Dean III	President Nixon's lawyer
Representative Robert Drinan	Member of House Judiciary Committee; offered resolution to impeach Nixon
John D. Ehrlichman	Assistant to the President for Domestic Affairs
Daniel Ellsberg	Leaked "Pentagon Papers," secret report on the Vietnam War, to the press
Senator Sam Ervin	Chairman of the Senate Watergate Committee
Lewis Fielding	Daniel Ellsberg's psychiatrist
Gerald R. Ford	40th Vice President of the United States; 38th President
Virgilio Gonzalez	One of the Watergate burglars
L. Patrick Gray III	Acting Director of the Federal Bureau of Investigation (FBI)
Alexander Haig	White House Chief of Staff after Haldeman
H. R. (Bob) Haldeman	White House Chief of Staff
J. Edgar Hoover	Longtime Director of FBI
E. Howard Hunt	Charles Colson's aide, involved in Watergate burglary
Leon Jaworski	Second Watergate Special Prosecutor

Richard Kleindienst	Attorney General, appointed in 1972 after John Mitchell left to head Nixon's 1972 reelection campaign
G. Gordon Liddy	Former FBI agent, Committee to Reelect the President (CRP) employee, and mastermind of Watergate operation
Jeb Magruder	Top CRP official; testified against other White House aides
Eugenio Martinez	One of the Watergate burglars
James W. McCord	Head of security for CRP; a Watergate burglar
John N. Mitchell	Former Attorney General of the United States, managed Nixon's 1972 reelection campaign
Richard M. Nixon	37th president of the United States
Lawrence O'Brien	Chair of the Democratic National Committee
Elliott Richardson	Attorney General after Richard Kleindienst; resigned during Saturday Night Massacre
William Ruckelshaus	Acting Attorney General after Richardson resigned; also resigned during Saturday Night Massacre
James St. Clair	One of Nixon's attorneys in Watergate case
Judge John Sirica	Judge who heard Watergate case
Frank Sturgis	One of the Watergate burglars
Vernon Walters	Deputy Director of the Central Intelligence Agency (CIA)
Rose Mary Woods	President Nixon's secretary
Bob Woodward	*Washington Post* reporter who, with Carl Bernstein, first wrote about Watergate scandal.
Charles Alan Wright	One of Nixon's attorneys in Watergate case

Timeline of Events

November 5, 1968	Richard Nixon elected 37th president of United States
July 23, 1970	Nixon approves Huston Plan; later cancels plan
June 13, 1971	"Pentagon Papers" published in *New York Times* and *Washington Post*
June 17, 1972	Watergate break-in
November 7, 1972	Nixon reelected president
January 8-30, 1973	Watergate burglary trial
February 7, 1973	Senate votes to establish Watergate Committee
March 23, 1973	Judge Sirica reads McCord's letter at sentencing
April 30, 1973	Resignations of Haldeman, Ehrlichman, Kleindienst
May 17, 1973	Senate Watergate Committee begins hearings
May 18, 1973	Archibald Cox named Special Prosecutor
July 13, 1973	Alexander Butterfield reveals existence of tapes
July 23, 1973	Cox subpoenas nine tapes of White House meetings
July 25, 1973	Nixon refuses to turn over tapes
August 29, 1973	Sirica rules Nixon must turn over tapes
October 10, 1973	Vice President Agnew resigns
October 12, 1973	U.S. Court of Appeals upholds Sirica's ruling
October 12, 1973	Nixon nominates Gerald R. Ford as vice president
October 20, 1973	Saturday Night Massacre; Cox fired
November 1, 1973	Leon Jaworski named Special Prosecutor
April 11, 1974	House Judiciary Committee subpoenas 42 tapes
April 18, 1974	Jaworski subpoenas 64 tapes
April 29, 1974	Nixon says he'll release transcripts of tapes
May 24, 1974	Jaworski appeals to Supreme Court for ruling on tapes
July 24, 1974	Supreme Court rules Nixon must turn over tapes
July 27-30, 1974	Judiciary Committee passes articles of impeachment
August 9, 1974	Nixon resigns; Gerald R. Ford becomes president

Richard Nixon, center, celebrates with members of his team after winning the 1968 presidential election.

"I Have Impeached Myself"

Let us begin by committing ourselves to the truth, to see it like it is and tell it like it is, to find the truth, to speak the truth, and to live the truth.[1]

— Richard Nixon, accepting the Republican nomination in 1968

Dear Mr. Secretary:
I hereby resign the Office of President of the United States.[2]

— Richard Nixon, August 9, 1974

With these few words, Richard Milhous Nixon left his mark on history. Never before had a U.S. president resigned his post as leader of our nation before the end of his term. He had served his country as congressman, senator, vice president, and president. He was an articulate spokesman for the Republican party. He was a skilled negotiator in foreign affairs. But Nixon was brought down by his disregard for the law and a collection of secret tape recordings.

Between 1970 and 1973, the White House recorded over 4,000 hours of presidential conversations. Nixon never intended for anyone but himself to hear them. Only a few members of the White House staff knew they even existed. But in 1973, the White House staff was implicated in a series of crimes. Knowledge of the recordings became public. The tapes would help determine who was responsible for the crimes. Nixon's lawyers tried to keep the tapes from being used as evidence. However, the Supreme Court ruled in 1974 that Nixon would have to turn them over.

Their contents were shocking. The president was revealed as a profane, paranoid man. It was these conversations, once made public, that brought about his downfall. As Nixon observed, "I have impeached myself."[3]

CHAPTER ONE

Watergate Break-in

*I will never forget when I heard about
this . . . forced entry and bugging. I
thought, what in the hell is this? What is
the matter with these people? Are they
crazy? I thought they were nuts! A
prank!* [1]

— **Richard Nixon to John Dean,
February 28, 1973**

James W. McCord, Jr., was worried. The operation
was not going smoothly. The time was just after midnight, June 17, 1972. As a
former Central Intelligence Agency (CIA) agent, he was familiar with planting
"bugs." Modern electronic listening devices were tiny and could be easily
hidden. All he had to do was install one in the phone of Lawrence O'Brien,
chairman of the Democratic National Committee. But breaking into the DNC's
office was harder than expected.

Entering the Watergate office and apartment complex was easy. His men
had taped a door open in the basement of the downtown Washington, D.C.,

building earlier. But they couldn't pick the lock on O'Brien's office door upstairs. They ended up taking the door off its hinges.

What really worried McCord, though, were the radios. The static was so loud that they were forced to turn them off. They couldn't risk someone hearing and discovering their break-in. Without the radios, their lookout across the street couldn't warn them if there was trouble.

McCord's concern was justified. Downstairs, a security guard discovered the taped door. Fearing a burglary, he called the police. Soon the officers found five men hiding in the Democratic headquarters. The intruders didn't seem like typical burglars. They were middle-aged, wearing suits, and carrying cameras and electronic surveillance devices. Because of the sophisticated equipment, the police called the Federal Bureau of Investigation. The FBI handles violations of the nation's wiretapping laws.

The officers took the burglars to jail. They booked the five men for breaking and entering. The police were surprised when a lawyer showed up to represent the prisoners the next morning. None of the men had made any phone calls. How had the attorney known they were there? FBI agents soon found the answer.

E. Howard Hunt had watched the burglars' arrest from the hotel across the street. The FBI discovered that a key carried by one of the burglars fit Hunt's hotel room. The FBI began investigating him as well. Hunt's job had been to keep radio contact with G. Gordon Liddy, the boss of the Watergate operation.

It was Hunt's lawyer who had come to the jail. After seeing their attorney, the burglars admitted they had used false names. Besides McCord, there were Virgilio Gonzalez, Frank Sturgis, Eugenio Martinez, and Bernard Barker. When they appeared in court that day, the judge ordered them held without bail.

The Watergate office and apartment complex in Washington, D.C., where the
Democratic National Committee had its headquarters

The FBI agents were shocked to learn the identity of the culprits. The burglars were ex-CIA agents. McCord was head of security for the Committee to Reelect the President (CRP). Hunt was on the White House staff. He worked as an aide to Charles Colson, one of President Richard Nixon's attorneys. The FBI had not yet linked Liddy, a former FBI agent himself, to the burglary.

Liddy knew that it was important to hide the White House connection to the burglary. Nixon was running for reelection, and the voters would choose the next president in November. Spying on the opposing party wasn't unheard of. But burglarizing the Democrats' office would make very bad publicity. He called Jeb Magruder, a top CRP official. Magruder consulted with John Mitchell, who had resigned as attorney general in March 1972 to head CRP. Magruder told Liddy to contact the new attorney general, Richard Kleindienst. The attorney general heads the Department of Justice.

Liddy asked Kleindienst to free McCord from jail. With McCord out of the way, perhaps the connection with CRP could be concealed. The attorney general angrily refused. He would not take part in a cover-up.

John Dean, chief counsel for the president, met with Liddy two days later. He needed to know how bad the situation was. Dean had assigned Liddy to work with CRP. Liddy assured him that none of the burglars would admit their association with the committee.

The next day, Dean met with the president. Nixon's secret tape recordings later revealed what happened at their meeting. The president was angry that the CRP agents had made such a blunder. But the damage was done. They considered their options. The White House could admit responsibility and accept the consequences. There would be much bad publicity for the Republicans. But it wasn't necessarily fatal to the reelection campaign. Perhaps the Democrats could be exposed in similar exploits.

Finally, though, Nixon decided to do otherwise. "Just stonewall it,"[2] he told his aides. They would admit no knowledge of the burglars' actions. The presidential election was only five months away. The break-in would have to be concealed at least until then.

Nixon was afraid that other political crimes would be exposed if word got out about the burglary. This was not the first covert operation for the burglars. They had begun their mischief during Nixon's first term as president, from 1969 to 1972.

Four of the seven Watergate defendants gather outside a Washington, D.C., courtroom with their lawyer, attorney Henry Rothblatt, in January 1973. From left to right they are: Virgilio Gonzalez, Frank Sturgis, Eugenio Martinez, Rothblatt, and Bernard Barker.

Responding to protests against the Vietnam War, the White House staff had developed a secret plan to gather information on groups they considered subversive. The Huston Plan authorized break-ins, wiretaps, opening mail, and infiltrating groups by the CIA, the FBI, and military intelligence. The author of the plan, Tom Charles Huston, had warned the president that these actions were clearly prohibited.

Nixon had approved the plan anyway, on July 23, 1970, but canceled it a few days later. Attorney General Mitchell and J. Edgar Hoover, director of the FBI, had refused to go along with the illegal plan.

In June 1971, the *New York Times* and the *Washington Post* began to print excerpts of the "Pentagon Papers." This was a secret report on the Vietnam War ordered in 1967 by the secretary of defense, Robert McNamara. One of the authors of the report was Dr. Daniel Ellsberg. He had given copies to the newspapers without permission. He hoped public knowledge of the contents would shorten the war. The documents revealed that the American people had been misled about Vietnam for three decades. Even Congress had been lied to about the conduct of the war.

The Justice Department demanded that the papers stop printing the excerpts. Dr. Ellsberg was charged with espionage. The department claimed national security was endangered. The government sought a court order to stop the publication of the documents. By the end of the month, the Supreme Court had ruled in the newspapers' favor. The cases were known as *New York Times v. United States* and *United States v. The Washington Post*. The court ruled the First Amendment protected the newspapers' right to publish the papers. The Justice Department would have to allow the articles to continue.

Nixon resorted to underhanded tactics against Dr. Ellsberg. His staff set up a special group of former CIA agents to investigate, and stop, news leaks. The "Plumbers," as they were known, broke into the office of Dr. Lewis Fielding,

Ellsberg's psychiatrist. G. Gordon Liddy supervised the burglary. He hoped to find confidential files that would discredit Ellsberg publicly. Perhaps Ellsberg had told his doctor that he was a Communist or that he used drugs. However, they found nothing. Dr. Fielding had removed Ellsberg's files from his office.

The Plumbers soon found other work with CRP. As the 1972 campaign season approached, Nixon's aides made plans for his reelection. CRP didn't confine its activities to traditional political tactics. It collected more than $50 million in contributions from individuals and corporations. Campaign laws strictly limit the amount of money that can be donated to politicians. Many of the gifts to CRP were illegal. The donors expected special favors from the government in return. Some of the money was "laundered." The donations were deposited in Mexican banks and withdrawn as cash to hide where they came from.

One reason the White House tried to stonewall the Watergate incident was to hide the source and uses of the illegal funds. CRP used the money to pay for "dirty tricks" against Nixon's opponents. People were hired to dig up embarrassing secrets about candidates and start false rumors. Spies were planted in Democratic campaign organizations. Edmund Muskie was one of the top Democratic contenders. CRP sent one of its men to work as Muskie's chauffeur. CRP also spread ugly rumors about Muskie's wife. Muskie was so upset at this that he cried at a news conference where he denied the stories. People worried about his emotional stability. A short while later, he withdrew from the race.

The White House ordered the Internal Revenue Service to audit the finances of prominent Democrats. Even though it is part of the executive branch, the IRS is forbidden to play partisan politics. Individuals' tax records are confidential. Even the president needs court permission to look at them legally.

CRP funds were also used to attack anyone who might embarrass the president. When antiwar rallies were held near the White House in May 1971, H. R. "Bob" Haldeman, Nixon's chief of staff, planned a response to the protest. That response included plans to hire Teamsters Union "thugs" to assault the demonstrators. According to the secret tapes, Nixon said he hoped the thugs would "go in and knock their heads off."[3]

One of CRP's schemes was codenamed Gemstone. G. Gordon Liddy detailed the Gemstone plan of attack to John Mitchell. The Democratic National Convention was to be bugged—electronic listening devices secretly installed. CRP would pay call girls to lure Democratic candidates to motels where they could be photographed. Protest leaders at the Republican Convention were to be beaten or kidnapped. Mitchell said that this was "not quite what I had in mind." He told Liddy to come up with a plan that was less expensive and more "realistic."[4]

CRP's "realistic" plan began right after Memorial Day in 1972. The Plumbers broke into the offices of the DNC in the Watergate complex. They copied files and installed wiretaps on some of the telephones. Early on the morning of June 17, they returned to the DNC. This time they were caught in the act.

CHAPTER TWO

Cover-up

What really hurts in matters of this sort is not the fact that they occur, because overzealous people in campaigns do things that are wrong. What really hurts is if you try to cover it up.[1]

— Richard Nixon, news conference,
August 30, 1972

By June 20, the Watergate case had become national news. Lawrence O'Brien, chairman of the Democratic National Committee, claimed that the burglary had "a clear line to the White House."[2] The Democrats filed a $1 million lawsuit against CRP. Newspapers began referring to the Republican committee as CREEP. Nixon met with the press on June 22. He announced that the "White House has had no involvement whatever in this particular incident."[3]

The next day, Nixon met with his chief of staff. The secret tapes recorded a far different story from the one told at the press conference. Haldeman reported to Nixon that the FBI's probe was getting too close to the truth. J. Edgar Hoover, longtime director of the FBI, had died some weeks before. Nixon

19

had appointed L. Patrick Gray as temporary director. Nixon and Haldeman hoped Gray could stop the Watergate investigation.

Haldeman suggested that Vernon Walters, deputy director of the CIA and an old friend of Nixon's, could help. Walters could claim that the FBI's Watergate probe was threatening national security by exposing a CIA operation. "The way to handle this now," Haldeman told Nixon, "is for us to have Walters call Pat Gray and just say, 'Stay the hell out of this—this is business here we don't want you to go any further on it.'"[4]

The "business" they were hiding was illegal campaign contributions. One of the burglars was carrying $100 bills traceable to campaign money laundered in Mexico. Nixon agreed. He told Haldeman to tell Gray, "Don't go any further into this case, period."[5] The tapes rolled on, recording the incriminating words.

Walters asked Gray to delay the investigation. The CIA did have a Mexican operation in progress. But Walters found there was no connection between that and the money-laundering scheme. The FBI probe would not affect the CIA operation. The FBI resumed its investigation into the burglary.

Meanwhile, the White House expanded its cover-up. Nixon's aides thought that the probe might implicate John Mitchell. Haldeman believed that Mitchell was told of the break-in beforehand. "I don't think he knew the details, but I think he knew,"[6] Haldeman told Nixon. Nixon thought it would be best if Mitchell stepped down as head of CRP. Claiming family problems, Mitchell resigned on the first of July.

John Dean arranged to have money from Nixon's secret campaign fund smuggled to the burglars through Hunt's lawyer. The "hush money" was supposed to pay their legal fees and support their families while they were in jail. In reality, it was to ensure that they would not reveal their connection with CRP. The burglars received more than $200,000 in the next three months.

The press worked hard to link the White House with the break-in. Two

Watergate co-conspirator G. Gordon Liddy

reporters for the *Washington Post*, Bob Woodward and Carl Bernstein, searched diligently for clues in the mysterious case. In August, they discovered that some of CRP's campaign funds had been deposited in the bank account of Bernard Barker, one of the burglars. The General Accounting Office (GAO) asked the Justice Department to look into the possibility of money-laundering. The reporters traced phone calls made between Barker and G. Gordon Liddy, tying the ex-FBI man and employee of CRP to the plot for the first time. The *Post* also reported that Haldeman and Mitchell, while he was still attorney general, controlled reelection funds. Government officials aren't allowed to work for political candidates.

Despite the news stories, the cover-up seemed to be working as the election

James W. McCord, the former Nixon campaign security coordinator who was arrested in the Watergate break-in, poses outside the U.S. District Court in Washington, D.C., before his trial in January 1973.

approached. Although the Democrats tried to make the most of the new disclosures, they made little headway. Nixon was nominated by the Republican party for a second term. Questioned by the press about Watergate, Nixon replied, "I can state categorically that [our] investigation indicates that no one on the White House staff, no one in this administration, presently employed, was involved in this very bizarre incident."[7]

The burglars' case was prosecuted by the Justice Department before a federal grand jury. A grand jury is a panel of citizens who hear evidence of a crime to decide if it should go to trial. Grand jury proceedings are kept secret from the public. In September, the five burglars plus Liddy and Hunt were indicted—they would have to stand trial.

Despite the increasing negative publicity, Nixon won the election in November by a landslide. The public saw his opponent, Senator George McGovern, as too liberal, too soft on crime, and a weak leader. Aside from Vietnam, they were impressed with Nixon's achievements in foreign affairs. McGovern lost every state but Massachusetts.

The burglars' trial began on January 8, 1973, in the U.S. District Court for the District of Columbia. Hearing the case was Chief District Judge John Sirica. The prosecutors contended that Liddy had planned the break-in. They said he had misspent the money given him by CRP for legitimate political purposes. This was what CRP officials had told the Justice Department. Magruder said as much at the trial. Although Liddy pleaded not guilty, he didn't deny the story.

All the others charged in the burglary, except McCord, pleaded guilty. At their trial, none of the defendants testified. They had all secretly been assured presidential pardons if they accepted short prison terms. The president had not agreed to this. His aides had made the promise to buy the burglars' silence.

Sirica tried to pry the truth out of the men. "Now, in your own words," the judge told Hunt, " I would like you to tell me from the beginning just how you got into this conspiracy, what you did, various things that you did, so I can decide whether or not you are knowingly and intentionally entering this plea voluntarily with full knowledge of possible consequences."[8] Sirica asked the defendants if they were being paid to keep quiet. No one would talk. Finally he was forced to accept the guilty pleas.

McCord and Liddy's trial was no more revealing. Neither man testified in his own defense. The jury convicted both men on January 30. Judge Sirica was unhappy. "I am still not satisfied that all the pertinent facts that might be available . . . have been produced,"[9] he told the court. Sirica hoped that the "pertinent facts" would still come out. He set sentencing for all the Watergate defendants for March 23.

Public interest in Watergate was still low. Nixon's landslide win in the elections made a minor political ploy like the Watergate bugging seem unimportant. Congress wanted to know more, however. CRP's shady financing had drawn the attention of the House Banking and Currency Committee the previous summer. The committee's investigation found evidence of deeper corruption. On January 11, the Justice Department charged CRP with campaign-financing violations.

Democratic legislators pressed for a deeper probe into the connection between CRP and the Watergate burglars. Republicans reluctantly went along to avoid the appearance of partisanship. On February 7, the Senate created a special committee to investigate Watergate. It was called the Senate Select Committee on Presidential Campaign Activities. The committee, known as the Watergate Committee, began preparing for public hearings. The stage was set for the biggest confrontation between Congress and the president in generations.

A development in another area marked the first skirmish between the two

Acting FBI Director L. Patrick Gray III prepares for a hearing before the Senate Judiciary Committee in March 1973.

branches of the government. The Senate confirmation hearings of L. Patrick Gray for director of the FBI led to a pitched battle over the president's right to withhold information. This was the issue that was to be at the heart of the Supreme Court case that decided President Nixon's fate.

Major presidential appointments must be approved by the Senate. On February 28, senators began asking Gray about the FBI's probe of the Watergate case. Gray disclosed that John Dean had taken part in the investigation. This seemed to be a conflict of interest, since the White House might have been implicated. The Senate asked Dean to testify. Nixon informed the Senate that neither Dean nor any other of his aides would appear before Congress. He claimed that the Constitution gave him executive privilege to prevent their testimony.

When the nation's founders created the U.S. Constitution, they feared that future leaders might try to restrict the rights of the citizens. To discourage this, they divided power among three branches of the government. This is called separation of powers.

The executive, legislative, and judicial branches were created as independent forces. The executive branch consists of the president and his or her administration. The president controls the armed forces, the cabinet, and various subordinate government departments. The legislature branch is made up of the Senate and House of Representatives and their staffs. The judiciary branch includes the Supreme Court and all the minor courts.

Each branch has specific duties. The other branches cannot interfere with those duties, except as allowed by the Constitution. In particular, the legislature makes laws, the judiciary interprets the laws, and the executive enforces them. There are checks and balances among the branches. Judicial appointments are made by the president and confirmed by the Senate. The executive's Department of Justice brings federal criminal cases before the courts. And a person convicted by the court can always be pardoned by the president.

Laws passed by Congress must be signed by the president. He or she may choose to veto the law by refusing to sign it. Congress may overcome the veto if both houses pass the law by at least a two-thirds vote. The courts, in turn, may rule that the law is unconstitutional.

The president is also answerable to Congress. The Senate must approve the president's appointments to the cabinet and other important posts. Congress can withhold the funds to run the president's administration. In serious cases, legislators can impeach the president and remove him or her from office. To impeach a president, that is, to bring him or her to trial before the Senate, is a major undertaking. It requires a vote by a majority of the House of Representatives. Trial is held before the Senate, with the chief justice of the Supreme Court presiding. Two-thirds of the Senate must agree to remove the president from office.

Nixon used the separation of powers doctrine to argue that Congress couldn't force Dean to testify. He claimed that would interfere with the proper functioning of the executive branch. If his aides were required to reveal presidential secrets, he said, it would deny him the "absolute confidence in the advice and assistance offered by the members of his staff."[10] Furthermore, Dean was his attorney. As such, he was covered by the "lawyer-client" privilege. Attorneys are required not to reveal conversations between themselves and their clients.

The Senate backed down but was still critical of this use of executive privilege. It seemed as though Nixon had something to hide. Nixon denied this and claimed he was only protecting the power of the presidency. "Executive privilege will not be used as a shield to prevent embarrassing information from being made available but will be exercised only in those particular instances in which disclosure would harm the public interest,"[11] he declared.

CHAPTER THREE

Cover-up Exposed

I want you all to stonewall it, let them plead the Fifth Amendment, cover up or anything else, if it'll save it—save the plan.[1]

— **Richard Nixon to John Mitchell and H. R. Haldeman March 22, 1973**

The burglars' trial drew to a close. The defendants were worried. Soon they would be sentenced for their crimes. Sirica was known as "Maximum John" because of his stiff sentences. Given their refusal to talk, the burglars could hardly expect leniency. There was no sign of any presidential pardons. Hunt demanded another $120,000 to stay quiet.

It was McCord who finally broke. On March 20, he sent a letter to Sirica, promising to cooperate. He wrote that the defendants had been pressured to stay quiet. Witnesses at the trial had committed perjury, he said; that is, they lied under oath. He also said that other government officials were involved in the break-in. Sirica was elated. "This is going to break this case wide open,"[2] he told his clerk. Perhaps now he could get to the bottom of the mystery surrounding Watergate.

Judge John J. Sirica in his office in 1974

The next day, Nixon met with his attorney. Dean was nervous. He had been involved from the beginning. He knew he had committed illegal acts. It seemed like the truth would have to come out eventually. Things were beginning to spin out of control. "We have a cancer within, close to the Presidency, that is growing,"[3] he told Nixon. Dean reviewed the events of Watergate starting with the planning stages of the wiretapping. Then he discussed Hunt's request for more money.

"Basically," he told the president, as the secret tapes whirred, ". . . we are being blackmailed."[4] Dean was afraid that the demands would be never-ending. Nixon wanted to know how much money would be needed to keep the burglars quiet. Dean guessed a million dollars in the next two years. "We could get that. . . . You could get it in cash. I know where it could be gotten,"[5] the president said. Later in their talk, Nixon asked about Hunt's current demand. "That's why for your immediate things you have no choice but to come up with the $120,000, or whatever it is. Right?"[6] Dean agreed. "Get it,"[7] Nixon told him. Hunt's attorney received $75,000 that night.

It was too late to buy silence from McCord, though. Judge Sirica read McCord's letter in court on March 23. McCord reported that Mitchell, Dean, Colson, and Magruder all knew of the Watergate break-in before it happened. This was the crucial information that the Watergate investigators needed.

As John Dean later put it, "The dam was cracking."[8] The wire services carried the story, and public interest soared. The grand jury that indicted the burglars reconvened to consider the new evidence. They would be impaneled until December 1974, sitting longer than any other grand jury in U.S. history. The next week, McCord appeared before the Senate Watergate Committee. He repeated to Committee Chairman Sam Ervin and the others what he had told Sirica.

Dean now knew that the cover-up was doomed. He decided to tell the truth.

Senator Howard Baker, Jr., R-Tennessee, left, and Senator Sam J. Ervin, Jr., D-North Carolina, chairman, confer during a hearing of the Senate Watergate Committee in July 1973.

He hired a lawyer and began telling his story to the Watergate prosecutors. By cooperating, Dean hoped to be granted immunity and spared a prison sentence.

Magruder was the next to break the code of silence. He suspected that the federal prosecutors knew of his perjury at the burglars' trial. Magruder struck a deal with the prosecutors. He would testify against Mitchell, Dean, and Liddy. In return, they would recommend a lenient sentence.

Nixon met with Dean on April 16. He knew that Dean had started talking. The president asked his counsel to submit his resignation. Dean suspected that he was going to be blamed for the whole caper. He refused to resign unless Haldeman and John Ehrlichman, another top Nixon aide, also left.

The next day, Nixon announced that he would now allow his aides to testify instead of claiming executive privilege. He also declared that they should not be granted immunity in exchange for testimony. Nixon wanted Dean to know that he would have to pay for his part in Watergate. Dean threatened to involve the president if he was not granted immunity. "We will bring the President in—not in this case but in other things,"[9] Dean's lawyer told Assistant Attorney General Henry Petersen.

One of the "other things" was White House involvement in the Fielding break-in. At Ellsberg's trial, in March 1973, the burglary of his psychiatrist's office was revealed. Judge John Byrne dismissed the case against Ellsberg. The judge believed that the Plumbers' actions were illegal. The Justice Department began looking further into the Fielding break-in.

By the end of the month, Haldeman and Ehrlichman were in trouble. Nixon was reluctant to let his top aides go. He had promised that he would protect them. But it was evident that soon they would be indicted for criminal conspiracy to cover up the burglary. Both Dean and Magruder had exposed Haldeman and Ehrlichman's role in the cover-up to the Watergate prosecutors. Nixon demanded they leave in order to save him further embarrassment.

Nixon was afraid that his two closest confidants might turn against him to save their own necks. Once they stepped down, executive privilege could no longer shield them. Ehrlichman had told the president that he would have to start answering questions. The tapes reveal that Nixon responded in typical fashion. "Let me ask you this, to be quite candid," he said. "Is there any way you can use cash?"[10] Haldeman and Ehrlichman thought that would add to the problem.

The president appeared on national television on April 30. "Today, in one of the most difficult decisions of my presidency, I accepted the resignations of two of my closest associates in the White House—Bob Haldeman, John Ehrlichman—two of the finest public servants it has been my privilege to know,"[11] he announced.

Nixon also announced the resignation of John Dean. In reality, the president had fired him. He knew that Dean's testimony would be most damaging. Nixon hoped that Dean's lack of immunity would keep him from saying too much. He thought Dean probably wouldn't want to incriminate others if it would add to his own jail time. Judge Sirica granted Dean limited immunity. He would not be charged with the crimes he admitted to the Senate. However, any further evidence could be used against him.

Richard Kleindienst also stepped down. He had already decided to resign when Nixon asked him to leave. His close personal and professional relationship with Nixon's aides had compromised his position as attorney general.

The American public was outraged at the depth of corruption in the Nixon administration. The Justice Department could no longer be trusted to conduct the probe. Kleindienst's replacement, Elliot Richardson, appointed Archibald Cox as special prosecutor. Cox, a government outsider, was promised independence. It was his job to ferret out the facts in the case and present them to the grand jury.

On May 17, 1973, the day before the special prosecutor was appointed, the Senate opened its hearings to the public. The nation watched, fascinated, as the story unfolded on the evening news. McCord, Barker, and Magruder spun a tale of intrigue and espionage. They claimed they acted out of patriotism. They believed their actions were a defense against similar "dirty tricks" by the Democrats. None of the burglars questioned the illegal nature of their acts. After all, John Mitchell, who had been the nation's highest law enforcement agent before taking the job as head of CRP, had approved. Magruder admitted that he had lied at the burglars' trial. He blamed the atmosphere of civil disobedience rampant at the time.

Mitchell, Haldeman, and Ehrlichman continued to profess their innocence on the stand. As Dean had guessed, they put most of the blame on him. Ehrlichman said he considered the Fielding break-in as "well within the President's inherent constitutional powers."[12]

He cited the Communications Act of 1934, which mentioned "the constitutional power of the president to take such measures as he deems necessary to protect the United States against the overthrow of the Government . . . or against any other clear and present danger to the structure or existence of the Government."[13]

John Dean was the star witness. He faced a committee made up of four Democratic and three Republican senators. Dozens of senatorial staff members scurried around. A battery of television cameras recorded the scene. Chairman Ervin, a folksy, conservative Democratic senator from North Carolina, brought the meeting to order. The president's former counsel began his story.

Dean spent the first day of his testimony reading a 245-page statement describing his part in the scandal. Dean believed that the excesses of Watergate stemmed from the president's paranoia. Nixon thought that Democrats, liberals, and antiwar demonstrators were out to get him. Dean revealed that

Former White House aide John Dean III studies a memo from John J. Caulfield, another former White House aide, before giving testimony to the Senate Watergate Committee in June 1973.

Nixon had an "enemies list" of politicians, civic leaders, the press, and even movie stars. The public was disgusted that the White House used the FBI, the CIA, and the IRS against these law-abiding citizens. In particular, the CIA was forbidden by the National Security Act of 1947 to join in domestic security operations.

Dean's testimony brought other crimes to light. He told the Senate committee about the existence of the Huston Plan and the formation of the Plumbers. He revealed Ehrlichman's involvement in the Fielding break-in. Details of Liddy's Operation Gemstone were divulged.

Dean admitted his involvement with the early stages of the Watergate burglary. He told the horrified senators that former Attorney General John Mitchell had approved the clearly illegal break-in. All of the top staff had taken part in the cover-up.

Dean also revealed the destruction of evidence at Pat Gray's hands. As soon as E. Howard Hunt's involvement with the burglary was discovered, John Dean had examined the contents of Hunt's safe at the White House. He found incriminating documents relating to the Plumbers' activities and illegal campaign finances. Dean asked Ehrlichman what to do with the documents.

"Deep-six" them, Ehrlichman had advised, according to Dean. "You drive across the river on your way home at night, don't you?" Ehrlichman asked Dean. "Well, when you cross over the bridge on your way home, just toss the briefcase into the river."[14]

Dean had thought that was a clear case of obstructing justice. He turned the papers over to Gray. Gray burned them. Dean revealed this during his initial talks with the federal prosecutors in mid-April. Gray admitted the charges to Assistant Attorney General Petersen, claiming he never read the papers.

Nixon had already withdrawn Gray's name from consideration for FBI director. By allowing Dean to be present when the Watergate suspects were interviewed, Gray had destroyed any chance of his confirmation by the Senate. While a replacement was sought, though, he was allowed to remain as acting director. Some details of the destruction of evidence leaked out in late April, before Dean's Senate testimony. Nixon forced Gray to resign immediately.

Near the end of Dean's testimony, he told the senators of a meeting with Nixon on April 15, 1973. Dean had told the president that he was talking with the federal prosecutors. Nixon began asking "leading questions, which made me think that the conversation was being taped,"[15] Dean told the committee. He urged the senators to find out if there really was a tape. The committee didn't give much credence to Dean's theory. But they did begin asking witnesses if they were aware of any tapes of presidential conversations. As a result, the senators soon uncovered their most important piece of evidence.

By now, it appeared that Nixon was possibly implicated in the crimes exposed by the Senate committee. Senator Howard Baker asked the question on everyone's minds: "What did the president know, and when did he know it?"[16] Only Nixon could answer that question. The Senate could not force the president to testify. It appeared that impeachment might be the only recourse. Only then would executive privilege fail to protect Nixon from giving testimony. But then a simpler way to arrive at the truth presented itself.

Alexander Butterfield was a deputy assistant to H. R. Haldeman. When he was called to testify before the Senate, he revealed a surprising fact. In 1970, Nixon had a tape-recording system installed in the president's Oval Office in the White House. When Nixon was in the room, the system would automatically record any conversations there. The Executive Office Building across the street was likewise equipped. Very few people knew about the system. Only Haldeman, Ehrlichman, Butterfield, a few Secret Service agents, and the president himself were in on the secret.

After months of stonewalling and reluctant witnesses, here was a major breakthrough. Tapes of presidential conversations would provide indisputable evidence as to "what the president knew."

News of the taping system made headlines worldwide. Foreign diplomats and heads of state were disturbed that their discussions with the U.S. president might become public knowledge. Senators and congressmen were equally concerned. Representative Robert Drinan proposed impeaching Nixon.

The public was intrigued that the backroom politicking of the most powerful men in the world might soon be revealed. Actually, such taping had been conducted by other administrations, starting with Franklin Roosevelt's. However, this was not common knowledge at the time. Most people thought such secret taping was unethical.

Nixon stated that he had wanted to record events during his term of office for historical purposes. The tapes, he said, would assist him in writing his memoirs. Now and then, the tapes were helpful in conducting the routine business of the White House. But they also could prove who was telling the truth about Watergate.

Cox wanted the tapes and other records for the grand jury's use. When Nixon declined Cox's request, Judge Sirica ordered the president to turn over the requested materials to the grand jury. Nixon refused the court order.

The Senate committee also demanded the tapes. Nixon still refused, claiming executive privilege. But was he really entitled to withhold this evidence? This was the crucial issue in the Watergate affair. It would take a year and a decision by the highest court in the land to decide the question. And in the process, the roles of our three branches of government would be examined as never before.

CHAPTER FOUR

Battle for the Tapes

*The pending requests . . . would move us
from proper Presidential cooperation
with a Senate Committee to jeopardizing
the fundamental Constitutional role of
the Presidency. This I must and shall
resist.*[1]

—Richard Nixon, letter to
Senator Sam Ervin, July 6, 1973

In a letter to the Senate committee, Nixon gave his
reasons for rejecting the request to testify and open his records to the senators.
"My decision . . . is based on my Constitutional obligation to preserve intact the
powers and prerogatives of the presidency."[2] He mentioned the need for secrecy
in his discussions with his aides. Nixon cited the case of Harry Truman, who in
1953 had been ordered by the House Un-American Activities Committee
(HUAC) to appear before the committee. Truman had refused to comply,
"following a long line of precedents, commencing with George Washington
himself in 1796."[3]

Nixon attached a copy of Truman's letter to his own. Truman had listed the past presidents who had refused similar congressional requests. Besides Washington, the list included Jefferson, Monroe, Jackson, Tyler, Polk, Fillmore, Buchanan, Lincoln, Grant, Hayes, Cleveland, Coolidge, Hoover, and both Roosevelts. Truman's letter cited a report of the House Judiciary Committee of the forty-fifth Congress, dated March 3, 1879.

> The executive is as independent of either house of
> Congress as either house of Congress is independent
> of him, and they cannot call for the records of his
> actions, or the actions of his officers against his
> consent, any more than he can call for any of the
> journals or records of the House or Senate.[4]

Truman went on:

> The President…would become a mere arm of the
> legislative branch of the Government if he would
> feel during his term of office that his every act
> might be subject to official inquiry and possible
> distortion for political purposes.[5]

Nixon concluded, "If I were to testify before the Committee, irreparable damage would be done to the Constitutional principle of separation of powers."[6] The president also pleaded his case on national television. On August 15, he told the public:

> If I were to make public these tapes, containing as
> they do blunt and candid remarks on many

different subjects, the confidentiality of the office of the president would always be suspect from now on. It would make no difference whether it was to serve the interests of a court, of a Senate committee, or the president himself—the same damage would be done to the principle, and that damage would be irreparable. Persons talking with the president would never again be sure that recordings or notes of what they said would not suddenly be made public.

No one would want to advance tentative ideas that might later seem unsound. No diplomat would want to speak candidly in those sensitive negotiations which could bring peace or avoid war. No senator or congressman would want to talk frankly about the congressional horse-trading that might get a vital bill passed. No one would want to speak bluntly about public figures, here and abroad.

That is why I shall continue to oppose efforts which would set a precedent that would cripple all future presidents by inhibiting conversations between them and those they look to for advice. The principle of confidentiality of presidential conversations is at stake in the question of these tapes.[7]

When Nixon refused the requests from Cox for his records, the special prosecutor took legal action. Cox asked Judge Sirica to issue a subpoena to the president. Sirica did so on July 23. A subpoena is a court order to appear before the court or produce evidence. Anyone refusing can be placed in jail. It was the first time a president had been subpoenaed since 1807.

Senator Ervin's Senate committee also subpoenaed Nixon's records and tapes. The 1880 case of *Kilbourn v. Thompson* established that Congress has "the right to compel the attendance of witnesses and their answers to proper questions, in the same manner and by the use of the same means, that courts of justice can in like cases."[8] Congress had never tried to subpoena a president before.

Still Nixon refused to turn over the tapes. He was in no danger of being thrown in jail. As head of the executive branch, it was his job to enforce the law. Neither Congress nor the judiciary had a police force. Nixon maintained his previous stand. His cooperation, he said, would endanger the principle of separation of powers. He noted that he had waived executive privilege in allowing his aides to testify. However, their testimony could be limited to the issue before the committee. Written records, though, might mix relevant evidence with national security materials that must remain secret. It would be even more difficult to separate unrelated matters recorded on tape.

The subpoena Sirica issued for Cox made an interesting point. Cox said that by turning over the materials to him, Nixon would not jeopardize separation of powers. Cox, after all, was an employee of the executive branch. However, Nixon's new lawyer, Charles Alan Wright, disputed that. He pointed out that Cox claimed to be independent of the Justice Department. Besides, he intended to use the materials as evidence in criminal trials. This would involve a dispute between the executive and judicial branches.

Wright brought up the Jencks Act, passed by Congress in 1959. This law

Charles Alan Wright leaves U.S. District Court in Washington, D.C., after arguing against releasing the White House tapes relating to the Watergate affair in August 1973.

established that the government may refuse to provide court-ordered evidence if the need for confidentiality outweighed the need for punishment of the guilty. He also cited a Supreme Court case of 1953, *United States v. Reynolds.* The Court had held that the president's power to withhold documents came from "an inherent executive power which is protected in the constitutional system of separation of power." Wright claimed the "incremental advantage" of the tapes' evidence was not worth jeopardizing the "effective functioning of the presidency."[9]

Despite constitutional difficulties, Congress demanded to hear the tapes. Senator Ervin contended that executive privilege didn't extend to "either alleged illegal activities or political campaign activities."[10] Nixon's and Dean's statements were in direct conflict. Nixon claimed that he first learned of the cover-up from Dean on May 21, 1973. Dean said that they had discussed it on

September 15, 1972. There were many other discrepancies in the various witnesses' accounts.

Nixon continued to ignore Congress's subpoena. Judge Sirica was asked to force Nixon to comply. Eventually, Sirica ruled that he lacked jurisdiction. He said a judge could not order the president to obey an order from the legislative branch. However, the story was different for the subpoena he had issued for Cox.

Sirica issued another subpoena on behalf of Cox. He asked that the president either turn over the tapes or "show cause" why he wouldn't. Cox and Nixon's lawyers began preparing their arguments. Sirica was aware of the gravity of his order. He later wrote, "By signing the show-cause order, I had for the first time in our history begun a real test of the limits of a president's so-called 'executive privilege.' Other presidents had invoked the privilege, but no president had ever been challenged in court on its use."[11]

The lawyers argued their cases in district court on August 22, 1973. Wright repeated the reasoning used earlier in Nixon's letters to Congress and Cox. He pointed out that no court had ever before forced a president to comply with a subpoena. Impeachment was the only constitutional remedy available. Cox replied that no one was above the law. He challenged the president to either comply or "dismiss the case"—in other words, to fire him. If that happened, Cox said, "the people will know where the responsibility lies."[12]

At a news conference that day, Nixon announced he "would abide by a *definitive* decision of the highest court."[13] It seemed the president had already decided to appeal any decision against him. Actually, Sirica's decision a week later was a compromise. Rather than turn over the tapes to Cox, Sirica would examine them himself. By having Sirica hear the tapes in camera—that is, in private—national security concerns would be satisfied. Sirica would turn over only information relevant to the criminal cases. However, Nixon rejected the

President Nixon emphasizes a point during a press conference in Washington, D.C.

offer. He decided to take the case to the next highest court, the U.S. Court of Appeals.

Cox and Wright presented their arguments again before the U.S. Court of Appeals for the District of Columbia on September 11. The case was known as *Nixon v. Sirica*. The judges wanted to avoid a constitutional crisis. They asked the two sides to try to reach an out-of-court settlement. Neither side would budge.

Finally, on October 12, 1973, the court of appeals upheld Judge Sirica's order and told Nixon to turn over the tapes to him. Although the appeals court judges were sympathetic to the president's claims of executive privilege, they realized that some outside party had to examine the tapes. It was only common sense that a man couldn't judge his own case.

Vice President Spiro Agnew announces his resignation in an address to the nation on October 15, 1973.

Nixon was in a delicate position. Vice President Spiro Agnew had just resigned. He was accused of taking bribes while governor of Maryland. He had also been charged with not paying his taxes. Eventually, Agnew pleaded guilty to income tax evasion. Although Nixon had no connection with Agnew's troubles, it made his administration look bad.

Nixon had his own tax problems. In 1970, he had deducted almost a half million dollars from his income. He claimed that was the worth of the private papers he had donated to the National Archives. Formerly, such deductions had been allowed. Congress stopped the tax break in 1969. The IRS finally ruled that the president would have to pay the taxes owed. Nixon claimed the deduction was a mistake. His accountants were convicted later for the deduction. But meanwhile the incident provided more ammunition for his critics.

Meanwhile, in the Middle East, Egypt and Syria prepared to attack Israel. The Soviet Union was threatening to send troops to support the Arab nations. Nixon had been active in promoting peace in the region. By maintaining a balance of power in the area, he believed he was keeping the Soviets from gaining an advantage. On the other side of the world, U.S. troops were preparing for a big offensive in Vietnam. This was not a time to lose his political base at home.

Nixon was afraid that if an appeal to the Supreme Court went against him, his cause would be lost. After all, he had said that he would comply with a Supreme Court decision. He offered his own compromise. Instead of releasing the tapes themselves, he would provide a summary of their contents. He would allow Democratic senator John Stennis to listen to the tapes. That way, no one could accuse Nixon of hiding anything. However, Cox would have to promise not to subpoena any more tapes.

Cox didn't think much of the offer. Stennis was old and almost deaf. The summaries might not be accurate or complete. Besides, only original documents would be admissible as evidence in a criminal case. Nixon ordered Cox, as an employee of the executive branch, to accept the plan. Cox refused.

CHAPTER FIVE

Saturday Night Massacre

During my terms as President, justice will be pursued fairly, fully, and impartially, no matter who is involved. This office is a sacred trust, and I am determined to be worthy of that trust.[1]

— Richard Nixon, announcing appointment
of Elliott Richardson as Attorney General
April 30, 1973

Saturday, October 20, 1973, was a turning point in Richard Nixon's presidency. That morning, Cox appeared at a news conference. "I'm certainly not out to get the president of the United States,"[2] he began. He then outlined his reasons for refusing Nixon's compromise. Cox emphasized that his main concern was to uphold the process of law. He would not set a precedent by allowing anyone to ignore a subpoena.

Nixon saw Cox's actions as insubordination. He ordered the new attorney general, Elliot Richardson, to fire Cox. Richardson had seen the showdown

Special Prosecutor Archibald Cox details his objections to a proposed compromise on the release of the Watergate tapes during a news conference in Washington, D.C., on October 20, 1973.

49

coming for weeks. He had accepted the post of attorney general in the scandal-ridden administration on a condition. He was to be allowed complete independence in dealing with the special prosecutor. Now, Nixon had broken his promise. Richardson could not, in good conscience, go along with Nixon's order.

Richardson submitted his resignation to the president. Nixon appealed to him to wait at least until the Middle East crisis was resolved. He appealed to Richardson's sense of public duty. "I can only say that I believe my resignation is in the public interest,"[3] Richardson replied.

Nixon grudgingly accepted the resignation. The unpleasant task of firing Cox next fell on Deputy Attorney General William Ruckelshaus. Ruckelshaus likewise decided to quit. He refused to take part in an obvious attempt to obstruct justice. Nixon was furious. The White House announced that Ruckelshaus had been fired.

Third in command in the Department of Justice was Solicitor General Robert Bork. Bork hesitated to follow the president's order. Richardson convinced him to comply. The point had been made—firing the special prosecutor was an injustice. And if it wasn't Bork who gave the order, someone else would. Richardson told Bork that he should stay to provide support for Cox's staff. At least someone could continue the prosecution. Bork accepted the appointment as acting attorney general and fired Cox.

The White House announced the dismissals and resignation that night. The special prosecutor's office was to be abolished. The evening news showed footage of the FBI sealing the office. It seemed symbolic of the cover-up. The White House was determined to keep the truth about Watergate from coming out. As Richardson later said, "A government of laws was on the verge of becoming a government of one man."[4]

Nixon's actions came to be known as the Saturday Night Massacre. The public was outraged. News shows compared Nixon's actions to a military coup. "The country tonight is in the midst of what may be the most serious constitutional crisis in its history,"[5] reported an NBC anchorman. More than half a million telegrams flooded Washington in protest. Picketers marched outside the White House. Nixon's supporters in Congress abandoned him. Motions to impeach the president were introduced by congressmen of both parties.

The massive protests caught the White House by surprise. Nixon considered his dealings with the special prosecutor an internal matter. The Justice Department had been directed to continue the Watergate investigation. But the Saturday Night Massacre had done untold damage to his credibility. With the foreign wars demanding his attention, Nixon had to back down.

On October 23, as ordered by the court of appeals, Nixon's lawyers were back in Sirica's court. The subpoena for the tapes was due to be answered. Attorney Wright mentioned Nixon's attempt at compromise—to "end a constitutional crisis."[6] He said he believed the summaries would satisfy the conditions of the subpoena.

Then Wright surprised the court. He admitted that the events of the last few days could not be ignored. Clearly the public believed that Nixon was flouting the law. "This president does not defy the law, and he has authorized me to say he will comply in full with the orders of the court."[7] Wright said Nixon would turn over the tapes for in camera inspection by Judge Sirica before the end of the year.

Criticism for the firings barely abated. Congress debated passing a law to reinstate Cox. On October 26, Nixon announced that he would name a new special prosecutor. However, he would not allow access to any more tapes. White House summaries would have to do. Leon Jaworski was appointed on November 1. Jaworski was a Texas lawyer who had served on several government commissions. He was highly respected as fair and impartial.

Jaworski got right to work with Cox's remaining staff. They immediately encountered problems. Nine tapes had been subpoenaed. Those particular tapes were requested because of testimony of witnesses before the grand jury and the Senate. Dean, for example, reported that he had spoken with the president on the night of April 15, 1973. Dean said that they had discussed the Watergate cover-up on that date. The special prosecutor, therefore, asked for the tape of that conversation.

A week after agreeing to turn over the tapes, the White House announced that particular Dean tape didn't exist. Apparently, the recording device had run out of tape. The White House said another subpoenaed phone conversation between Nixon and Mitchell took place on a phone that wasn't monitored. Sirica suspected that Nixon was still hiding something.

The worst revelation was yet to come. A tape of a discussion between Haldeman and Nixon had been erased. Rose Mary Woods, Nixon's secretary, had been transcribing the tapes so they could be read by Sirica. She told the judge that she must have accidentally hit the record button when she tried to stop the machine to answer the phone.

Sirica had her reenact the scene. From her position, it appeared unlikely that was the cause of the erasure. What's more, she could account for only five minutes of the blank tape. Eighteen minutes had been erased. The entire conversation between Haldeman and Nixon involving Watergate had been on the erased tape.

Sirica asked the White House for an explanation. There was none. Reporters hounded Alexander Haig, the new chief of staff, about the erasure. "Perhaps some sinister force had come in and . . . taken care of the information on the tape,"[8] he replied.

Haig's comment drew derision around the country. It appeared the White House was grasping at straws. Many people believed that the "sinister force"

President Nixon's secretary, Rose Mary Woods, demonstrates how she could have accidentally erased a crucial conversation on one of the Watergate tapes.

was Nixon himself. Technical experts later reported that the tape had been erased at least five times over. It could hardly have been accidental.

Finally, the White House turned the tapes over to Sirica. After listening to the recordings, Sirica believed that Nixon was very much involved in the cover-up. Sirica turned over the relevant portions of the recordings to Jaworski. The special prosecutor agreed that things didn't look good for the president. The March 21 meeting between Nixon and Dean, in particular, seemed incriminating. Nixon's order for Dean to pay the blackmail money to Hunt seemed to confirm Sirica's suspicion that the president had taken part in the cover-up.

The grand jury now had all the evidence it needed. The jurors were ready to return indictments against Nixon's aides—and the president. Jaworski didn't believe it would be wise to indict Nixon. Constitutional law wasn't clear on how to charge a president with a crime. Jaworski thought that only the House of Representatives could make such charges, as part of the impeachment process.

The grand jury released its verdict on March 1, 1974. Indicted for conspiracy and obstructing justice were Mitchell, Haldeman, Ehrlichman, Colson, and three other aides. Nixon's name wasn't mentioned. But he had secretly been named as an unindicted co-conspirator. Although the jurors found Nixon as guilty in the cover-up as the rest, he wouldn't be charged.

Jaworski privately gave Sirica the evidence against Nixon. He urged Sirica to turn it over to the House for impeachment proceedings. After the indictments were returned, Sirica sent the documents to the House Judiciary Committee. The suitcase with the evidence arrived at the Capitol building under armed guard.

The Senate Watergate Committee had finished its hearings the previous year. Now it was up to the House Judiciary Committee to bring Nixon to task. The representatives would review the evidence, hold hearings, and decide whether to recommend impeachment to the full House. The House committee decided that more evidence was needed. The congressmen issued a subpoena for tapes of an additional 42 conversations.

Jaworski had already been trying to get the White House to release more evidence. The seven tapes he had were enough to indicate a crime but probably not enough to obtain a conviction. He asked for more tapes and other records. Some of the presidential papers had been requested months before. The White House was firm. The president would release nothing more. Finally Jaworski sent another subpoena for the papers and 64 more tapes.

President Nixon points to the transcripts of the White House tapes in April 1974 after he announced during a nationally televised speech that he would turn over the transcripts to the House impeachment investigators and make them public.

Nixon kept the special prosecutor and House committee waiting until April 29. Then he announced that he would release only transcripts of the tapes. White House personnel had copied only the information involving Watergate from the requested tapes. They would be provided to Jaworski, the House committee, and the general public as well. The transcripts rolled off the presses.

At last people could see for themselves just what had happened behind the scenes at the White House. *The Presidential Transcripts* sold millions of copies. What the public saw was hardly beneficial to Nixon's cause. Although the profanity had been removed from the transcripts, it was clear that Nixon was a vulgar man. "Expletive deleted" had been substituted frequently in the narratives. The president often made crude and racist remarks. And his contempt for the process of law was clear.

Nixon thought the transcripts would clear him. A White House summary tried to explain away the discussions of stonewalling and blackmail. Nixon had been merely thinking aloud, exploring various options, according to the summary. The president said he had sought to hide evidence of wrongdoing only from his political foes, not from the courts. No one found the excuses believable. The plan backfired.

Nixon's support declined even further. Republican leaders suggested that it would be best for the party, and the country, if he stepped down. Editorials in even the most conservative newspapers called for Nixon's impeachment. The public had lost confidence in his ability to perform his duties.

Jaworski and the House committee were not satisfied with the transcripts. They didn't trust that the transcripts were accurate or complete. No one but White House personnel had heard the tapes. Besides, transcripts would not be allowed in a criminal trial. The men charged in the grand jury's indictments deserved the best evidence possible. As House Speaker Carl Albert put it, "Why substitute other evidence when the direct evidence is available?"[9] The House committee and Jaworski continued to pressure the White House for the tapes themselves.

Nixon announced that he would refuse to comply with the House subpoena. The House Judiciary Committee viewed Nixon's refusal as further grounds for impeachment. Impeachment now was Congress's only recourse. Jaworski, on the other hand, had recourse in the courts. He began to pursue his case with Judge Sirica, just as Cox had done. The White House ordered Jaworski to stop, but he refused. This time, Nixon didn't dare to fire the special prosecutor.

Again, Sirica ruled that the special prosecutor's subpoena was valid. Nixon's attorney prepared to take the case before the appeals court once more. Jaworski decided that he needed to speed up the proceedings. The president's aides were going to trial in September. Jaworski wanted the tapes as evidence before then. Besides, the House Judiciary Committee would soon vote on impeachment. Congress should have the best possible evidence also.

Whichever side won, the case would probably be appealed to the Supreme Court. The Court normally heard cases only between September and May. Jaworski asked that the appeals court level be skipped. That way, the Supreme Court could hear the case before the justices' summer vacation.

It was rare for the Supreme Court to hear a case that hadn't come through the U.S. Court of Appeals. Nevertheless, the justices agreed to Jaworski's plea. They ordered the lawyers to appear on July 8, 1974, to present their oral arguments in *United States v. Nixon*. Meanwhile, the justices started examining the briefs submitted by the lawyers on both sides of the case. Briefs are the written arguments lawyers file with a court that support their case. The justices knew their decision would be among the most important in the history of the Court. Not only would it decide Nixon's fate, but it would set the limits of power for all subsequent presidents.

CHAPTER SIX

Presidential Powers

Respect for law in a nation is the most priceless asset a free people can have, and the Chief Justice and his associates are the ultimate custodians and guardians of that priceless asset. [1]

—Richard Nixon, announcing
Warren Burger's nomination as
chief justice, May 21, 1969

"Right on, Brother Dean!"[2] Thurgood Marshall cheered. The Supreme Court justice was watching a tiny black-and-white television in Justice Potter Stewart's office. John Dean had just implicated President Nixon at the televised Senate Watergate hearings.

Well-known for his court battles for school desegregation as a lawyer for the National Association for the Advancement of Colored People, Marshall was no fan of Nixon. The president had been impeding racial desegregation of the nation's schools. Marshall also objected to Nixon's campaign speeches attacking the Supreme Court. In his 1968 campaign, Nixon had criticized the Court's defense of individual liberties as coddling criminals. And as part of his

Justice Thurgood Marshall stands in front of the Supreme Court building.

"Southern strategy," Nixon had attempted to appoint two conservative, law-and-order judges to the Court. Congress refused to confirm their nominations.

Law clerks passing by the TV joined in. "You lie, you lie,"[3] they yelled at Nixon's defenders. Watergate was the talk of the courthouse in June 1973. The justices knew they might have to issue a ruling on some aspect of the case. When Nixon refused to honor the subpoenas for his tapes, it seemed certain that the Court would get involved.

Four of the Court's nine justices were apt to side with the president. Chief Justice Warren Burger and Associate Justices Harry Blackmun, Lewis Powell, Jr., and William Rehnquist had been appointed by Nixon. William Douglas, William Brennan, Stewart, and Marshall were not so sympathetic to the president. Byron White's views were never easily guessed.

Chief Justice Burger was no stranger to Nixon. He occasionally had lunch with the president. He had even sent a list of candidates for the first special prosecutor to the attorney general. When asked about Watergate in May 1973, he called the investigation a vindictive witch-hunt. Now, a year later, he wasn't so sure.

The Supreme Court met May 31, 1974, to consider Jaworski's request for a speedy hearing. The usual route to a Supreme Court hearing is to petition the court for a writ of certiorari. At least four of the justices must vote that a case merits a hearing in order for it to come before the Court. They then order that the certified records of the last court to hear the case be forwarded to them. Petitions for "cert" are almost always denied unless the case has been through the appeals process. Five justices must vote to allow a case to skip the appeals court and go directly to the Supreme Court. This has happened only a half dozen times in the history of the Court.

Only eight justices attended the meeting in the Court's book-lined conference room. William Rehnquist would not be involved in the case. Before

Watergate Special Prosecutor Leon Jaworski speaks with reporters outside the U.S. District Court in Washington, D.C., on May 16, 1974.

becoming a Supreme Court justice, Rehnquist had worked at the Justice Department. While there, he had drafted Nixon's original position on executive privilege. He had also worked closely with Mitchell and Ehrlichman. Ex-Attorney General Kleindienst was one of Rehnquist's closest friends. It would not be proper for him to sit on the case. Rehnquist disqualified himself.

Burger spoke first at the conference. It was customary for the chief justice to address the meeting first. Then the senior associate justice gave his opinion and on down the line. The justice who had been appointed most recently spoke last.

Burger told the justices he did not want the Court to get into the habit of skipping the appeals court. He could find no national emergency in this case. The only result he could see if they sent the case back to the lower court, he said, would be a delay in the trial of the president's aides. Burger said he didn't consider that serious. Nevertheless, he wasn't ready to cast his vote.

Douglas, upset at Nixon's disrespect for the law, argued that everyone had to turn over evidence. The defendants at the conspirators' trial deserved the best evidence available, he said. The case was bound to end up in Supreme Court eventually. It was best, he believed, to decide it quickly. He voted to hear the case.

Brennan spoke next. He believed there was an important constitutional issue at stake. Nixon's claim of absolute executive privilege had no merit, Brennan argued. It was the duty of the Court, he said, to take decisive action. He also voted to hear the case.

Stewart was concerned with the prestige of the Court. The press had been reporting that the Supreme Court would not get involved. Media commentators claimed that the tapes issue was a classic political dispute between two branches of the government. The Court had typically shied away from such matters.

If the Court's future decisions were to carry any weight at all, it must establish its authority now, Stewart said. Besides, Nixon's defiance could not be permitted. Stewart reminded his fellow justices of Nixon's pledge, made the previous August, to obey only a "definitive" opinion. Court rulings were to be obeyed, Stewart said, definitive or not. He did not think it was up to Nixon to decide whether to comply. Stewart voted to hear the case.

White did not think they should be arguing the merits of Nixon's case. The only question for now was whether they should bypass the appeals court. Other aspects of the case, he said, could wait. He didn't believe a few months' delay would hurt. White voted no.

Thurgood Marshall's vote was never in doubt. He considered Nixon to be morally unfit to be president. Watergate was merely the worst example of the man's abuses, according to Marshall. He was eager to put the president in his place. Marshall cast the fourth yes vote.

Blackmun believed the only reason to hear the case now was to prevent delay in the aides' trials. He concluded that was not crucial to the nation's well-being. He voted no.

One more vote was needed to allow the case to be heard. All eyes turned to Powell, the junior member. The Nixon appointee believed that Watergate qualified as a national emergency. Powell voted yes. Burger, seeing which way the wind blew, joined the yes votes. The Supreme Court would hear Nixon's case at once.

The Court began examining precedents set by past court cases on presidential powers. Most of these decisions had been considered by the appeals court the previous fall. The justices started researching the history behind the appeals court opinion.

They agreed that executive privilege was an important right to preserve. The problem was, executive privilege had never been defined. It wasn't mentioned in the Constitution. Presidents often claimed it, but the Court had

Supreme Court Chief Justice John Marshall, who served on the Court from 1801 to 1835

never set its limits or even accepted its validity. But most agreed the United States would have an ineffective president without it.

The appeals court decision in *Nixon v. Sirica* cited a case involving President Thomas Jefferson. Aaron Burr was Jefferson's first vice president. In *United States v. Burr*, the Court issued Jefferson a subpoena to turn over some of his private letters. The letters were to be used as evidence to support Burr's case against treason charges.

Jefferson ignored the order. Chief Justice John Marshall ruled that a subpoena may be issued to anyone, presidents included. Jefferson turned over the letters but did not fully comply with the subpoena. Marshall issued another opinion.

> The president, although subject to the general rules which apply to others, may have sufficient motives for declining to produce a particular paper, and those motives may be such as to restrain the court from enforcing its production. . . . I can readily conceive that the president might receive a letter which it would be improper to exhibit in public. . . . The occasion for demanding it ought, in such a case, to be very strong, and to be fully shown to the court before its production could be insisted on. . . . Such a letter, though it be a private one, seems to partake of the character of an official paper, and to be such as ought not on light ground to be forced into public view.[4]

The appeals court noted that Marshall's opinion didn't wholly support Nixon's case. The court was to respect the president's reasons for not producing records. But if the president's reasons were not strong enough, the appeals court stated, "the ultimate decision remained with the court."[5]

Before Watergate, the most important case involving presidential powers in modern times was *Youngstown Sheet & Tube Co. v. Sawyer* in 1952. The United States was involved in a "police action" in Korea. Congress hadn't declared war, but President Truman had sent thousands of troops overseas. Truman was determined to keep Communists from taking over Korea.

The country was still recovering from World War II. When the nation's steel mill workers went on strike for better wages, supplies for the troops were threatened. Truman declared a national emergency. Saying national defense was at stake, he directed the secretary of commerce, Charles Sawyer, to seize the steel mills.

The mills kept operating, but the owners brought suit against the secretary. They charged that the president was making law. This was a right that belonged to the legislature alone. Assistant Attorney General Holmes Baldridge argued the government's case in U.S. District Court before Judge David Pine. He claimed that Truman had acted within the scope of his powers as commander in chief and chief executive. Baldridge based the president's power "on Sections 1, 2, and 3 of Article 2 of the Constitution, and whatever inherent, implied, or residual powers may flow therefrom."[6]

Article 2 states, "The executive power shall be vested in a president of the United States of America."[7] Experts have argued that the vague statement meant only to clarify the title of our national leader. However, strong presidents have used it to justify vast powers.

Judge Pine didn't think that conditions warranted such drastic actions on Truman's part. The Korean action wasn't even a declared war. Baldridge contended that the president had unlimited powers in an emergency. In his view, the courts couldn't even decide what constituted an emergency. But

Baldridge noted there were limits on presidential power. "I do want to point out that there are two limitations on the executive power. One is the ballot box and the other is impeachment,"[8] he said.

Pine decided against Truman. He wrote that the Constitution defined "a government of limited, enumerated, and delegated power."[9] Nothing in Article 2 expressly gave the president the power to seize the mills. Truman couldn't justify his orders with "inherent" powers, the judge ruled. The president was restricted solely to his listed powers and duties. He could make treaties and grant pardons. He was commander in chief. He appointed judges, diplomats, and executive officers. He could convene or adjourn Congress. He was responsible for enforcing the nation's laws. That was the limit of his powers, according to Pine's decision.

Baldridge promptly took the case to the U.S. Court of Appeals. The Supreme Court deemed the case important enough to bypass the appeals court. The next time this would happen would be the *United States v. Nixon* appeal.

The Supreme Court upheld Judge Pine's decision. "The president's power, if any, to issue the order must stem either from an act of Congress or from the Constitution itself,"[10] Justice Hugo Black wrote for the Court. Resolution of labor conflicts was the province of Congress, not the president. The Court ordered the steel mills returned to their owners. Truman complied within a half hour of the order.

The appeals court judges in *Nixon v. Sirica* noted several other recent rulings that related to the Nixon case. In *Environmental Protection Agency v. Mink*, a citizen had sued to look at EPA records under the Freedom of Information Act. EPA officials withheld some records. The information sought by the plaintiff was mixed in with policy suggestions that were exempt from FOIA rules. This was similar to Nixon's contention that the evidence sought by the special prosecutor on the tapes was mixed in with other conversations. The

Former Attorney General John Mitchell, pictured above with pipe, asserted in another Supreme Court case that the government had the right to use wiretaps to protect the nation from subversive groups.

president's counsel had used this argument in his brief to the court in *Sirica*.

Recordings are the raw material of life. By their very nature they contain spontaneous, informal, tentative, and frequently pungent comments on a

variety of subjects inextricably intertwined into
one conversation. . . . The nature of informal,
private conversations is such that it is not practi-
cal to separate what is arguably relevant from
what is clearly irrelevant.[11]

The Court ruled that inspection of the EPA records by the judge in the case should be allowed. The judge reviewing the records could be relied on to maintain secrecy, the Court said.

Another Supreme Court case the *Nixon v. Sirica* judges considered was *United States v. United States Court for the Eastern District of Michigan*. This involved an antiwar group's attempt to bomb a CIA office in 1970. The government had used a wiretap to gather information on the plot. Lawyers for the defendants sued to obtain copies of the recordings to use for their defense. The prosecution presented an affidavit from Attorney General John Mitchell stating that the wiretaps were "necessary to protect the nation from attempts of domestic organizations to attack and subvert the existing structure of the government."[12]

District Court Judge Damon Keith ordered the Justice Department to provide the wiretap transcripts. The government insisted that it had the right to keep such affairs secret. "The power at issue in this case is the inherent power of the president to safeguard the security of the nation,"[13] it maintained.

The "Keith Case," as it became known, moved up to the Supreme Court. The justices agreed with Keith. The government should have obtained a court order before tapping the suspects, the Court ruled. Maintaining domestic security was a valid concern, the justices said. But it must be carried out "in a manner compatible with the Fourth Amendment."[14] The Fourth Amendment guarantees "the right of the people to be secure in their persons, houses, papers, and effects, against unreasonable searches and seizures."[15] The Court ordered the government to release the illegally tapped conversations.

In making their decision on the Watergate case, the Supreme Court justices considered two other cases. One was the *Reynolds* case, brought up by Nixon's attorney, Charles Wright. The Court had allowed the government to withhold evidence in a case because it involved military secrets. The need for secrecy was overriding. The defendant was allowed to go free rather than risk national security.

However, even if evidence could be suppressed, it still must be examined. In *Reynolds*, the Court wrote, "The court itself must determine whether the circumstances are appropriate for the claim of privilege."[16] That decision set a precedent for at least allowing a judge to review evidence to determine whether it risked national security.

The other case was *Committee for Nuclear Responsibility, Inc. v. Seaborg*, in which a federal official turned down a request for information from a citizens' group. The official, Glenn Seaborg, chair of the U.S. Atomic Energy Commission, then refused to comply with a court order to turn over the information, using separation of powers as an excuse. Once again, the Court ruled that it was up to the judiciary, not the executive, to determine whether evidence should be suppressed. The Court ordered Seaborg to release the information.

The Supreme Court ruling in *Seaborg* could easily apply to Nixon's case. The *Seaborg* opinion noted that if presidents or department heads could decide what evidence to release to the court, they could easily cover up corruption in their departments.

No executive official or agency can be given
absolute authority to determine what documents
in his possession may be considered by the court

in its task. Otherwise the head of an executive department would have the power on his own say-so to cover up all evidence of fraud and corruption when a federal court or grand jury was investigating malfeasance in office, and this is not the law.[17]

While the Supreme Court considered Nixon's case, the House readied a full attack on the president. Calls for impeachment had been growing since the Watergate scandal began. The House Judiciary Committee had been holding closed hearings since May 9, 1974, to consider impeachment. With the available evidence, Nixon's trial was no sure thing.

Few high officials had been impeached. In 1803, Federal Judge John Pickering was impeached and convicted for drunkenness and insanity. The need was obvious; there was little controversy. But other cases of impeachment had been political.

Supreme Court Justice Samuel Chase was impeached in 1804. The Federalist judge was accused of treating a political foe unfairly. He had tried a Jefferson supporter for sedition. President Jefferson's allies in Congress responded by putting Chase on trial. Chase's defense was that he hadn't been charged with an indictable crime. All the charges were merely political in nature. The Senate agreed; Chase was acquitted.

Andrew Johnson is the only president to have been impeached. Assuming the presidency after Lincoln's death, Johnson was not popular. He tried to be fair to the defeated Confederate states. The Republicans were a strong faction in Congress. They sought to punish the Southern people for the damages of the Civil War. When Johnson refused to go along, they impeached him.

The congressmen charged the president with 11 articles of impeachment.

Ten of them were indictable offenses. Johnson's impeachment and trial were still clearly political. No Democrats voted for impeachment or conviction. Only six Republican senators voted for acquittal. Johnson escaped conviction by one vote.

The charges against Nixon were certainly more than political offenses. Still, there were many reasons to avoid impeachment. An impeachment trial would be long and expensive. It would keep the president and Congress from attending to the nation's business. The country's national prestige would suffer. Foreign businesses and governments would hesitate to deal with an administration that might soon lose power in disgrace.

On the other hand, Nixon would still be free to conduct foreign policy while on trial. He had been making good progress in achieving peace with the U.S.S.R. and China and in the Middle East. With a sudden breakthrough, he might be hailed as a hero. Then the members of Congress pushing for impeachment would look petty and vindictive.

Many in the House were reluctant to vote for impeachment unless they were positive Nixon could be convicted. That might be assured if the subpoenaed tapes showed evidence of crimes committed by the president. Congress, and the nation, waited for the Supreme Court's decision on whether the tapes should be released.

Senators Howard Cannon, D-Nevada; Hugh Scott, R-Pennsylvania; and Robert Byrd, D-West Virginia, confer on proposed changes in the rules for impeachment trials in August 1974. The three senators served on the Senate Rules and Administration Committee during the Watergate hearings.

Members of the U.S. Supreme Court stand on the steps of the Court building in this July 1974 photo. From left: Chief Justice Warren E. Burger; Associate Justice William O. Douglas; Associate Justice William J. Brennan; Associate Justice Potter Stewart; Associate Justice Byron R. White; Associate Justice Thurgood Marshall; Associate Justice Harry A. Blackmun; Associate Justice Lewis F. Powell, Jr.; and Associate Justice William H. Rehnquist.

CHAPTER SEVEN

The Court Decides

I am gratified to note that the Court reaffirmed both the validity and the importance of the principle of executive privilege, the principle I had sought to maintain.[1]

— Richard Nixon press release
July 24, 1974

In informal talks among the justices, it soon became clear that Nixon's guilt was obvious to all. The evidence against the president was strong. The tapes already released revealed that Nixon had encouraged the cover-up. He had agreed to pay hush money to the burglars. He had advised his aides to withhold the truth from the grand jury. "You can say, 'I don't remember.' You can say, 'I can't recall,'"[2] Nixon had told Dean and Haldeman on the March 21 tape. The justices believed that the president was guilty of obstructing justice.

But they still needed justification to demand more tapes. They couldn't upset the balance of power among the branches of the government. On the one hand, Nixon should answer for his crimes. On the other hand, the Court did not want to hamper the ability of future presidents to carry out their duties.

Most on the justices' minds was the need for confidentiality. Presidents needed frank advice. The executive branch wouldn't be able to function effectively if aides had to watch their every word. As Stewart put it, "Government cannot function in a goldfish bowl."[3]

Even Marshall saw the need to preserve executive privilege. He favored a strong opinion against Nixon. But he didn't want to see his candid discussions with President Lyndon Johnson made public.

The justices argued over the authority of the subpoena to the president. This was contained in Rule 17(c) of the rules for criminal procedure for federal courts. The rule allowed the courts to subpoena anyone and anything. All that was needed was that the evidence or testimony be both admissable in trial and potentially relevant.

Powell believed that the courts should set a higher standard of need for subpoenas to presidents. Brennan and White saw no need to treat the president differently from any other American. They argued that Rule 17(c) was "adequate to protect the president from unnecessary interference or harassment."[4] The justices couldn't agree on this point. They put off further debate until after the oral arguments.

Cases are presented to the Supreme Court in two stages. First the opposing lawyers present their written arguments, or briefs. They cite rulings set by past Court decisions. The attorneys give reasons why those opinions, or precedents, should apply to the current case.

Next the Court schedules a hearing for oral arguments. Each side is usually given a half hour to summarize its position. The attorneys answer any questions the justices may pose to them. Defense and prosecution counsels may rebut each other's arguments. Strict time limits are observed. Lawyers may not have the chance to say all they planned. Time spent answering justices' questions is taken from their allotted half hour. The Court sometimes takes months after oral arguments to decide a case. In some cases, the Court asks the lawyers to present their cases a second time.

The time soon arrived for the hearing. Washington was astir as everyone tried to guess how the justices would rule. One hundred twenty seats are provided for the public during oral arguments. A day before the Nixon hearing was scheduled, people began lining up outside the ornate marble building that houses the Court. The proceedings started at 10:02 on July 8, 1974.

The justices deemed the case so important they allowed each side three hours for arguments. Jaworski led off by reciting the history of the case. He got as far as mentioning that Nixon was named an unindicted co-conspirator when he was interrupted.

Douglas wanted to know what relevance the grand jury finding had to the subpoena. "I thought that was primarily just for the knowledge, information of the House Judiciary Committee,"[5] he said. Jaworski indicated that he would be there whether or not Nixon had been named a conspirator. But, he said, the grand jury finding added weight to his argument for the tapes.

The special prosecutor continued with his presentation. There were no surprises. His arguments were the same ones he had offered to Judge Sirica. Cox had presented almost the same case to the appeals court. Jaworski finally presented his summary.

> This case really presents one fundamental issue.
> Who is to be the arbiter of what the Constitution
> says? . . . Now, the president may be right in how
> he reads the Constitution. But he may also be
> wrong. And if he is wrong, who is there to tell him

so? . . . This nation's constitutional form of
government is in serious jeopardy if the President,
any president, is to say that the Constitution
means what *he* says it does, and that there is no
one, not even the Supreme Court, to tell him
otherwise.[6]

James St. Clair argued for the defense. He did his best to present the case as a political issue. He claimed the Court shouldn't be involved in impeachment proceedings. Whatever the justices intended, their opinion would affect the House Judiciary Committee's decision on whether to recommend impeachment. "Well, those are none of our problems, are they?"[7] Douglas replied. Brennan pointed out that many decisions of the Court had political repercussions.

Marshall wanted St. Clair to acknowledge that the president would submit to the will of the Court. He had in mind Nixon's "definitive decision" statement. The counsel replied that he presented the legal question to the Court "for its guidance and judgment with respect to the law. The president, on the other hand, has his obligations under the Constitution."[8] In other words, Nixon would consider the Court's opinion advisory.

Powell posed another question. If the taped conversations involved a criminal conspiracy, would St. Clair still claim executive privilege? The lawyer said he would. "What public interest is there in preserving secrecy with respect to a criminal conspiracy?"[9] Powell asked. "A criminal conspiracy is criminal only after it's proven to be criminal,"[10] St. Clair replied.

Marshall jumped in. "If you know the president is doing something wrong, you can impeach him. But if the only way you can find out is [a subpoena], you can't impeach him, so you don't impeach him. . . . You lose me some place along

White House lawyer James St. Clair speaks to reporters on the steps of the Supreme Court building after arguing on behalf of President Richard Nixon.

there."[11] The audience laughed. Clearly, the Court was not buying St. Clair's circular logic.

The other half of the special prosecutor's team made the closing argument. Philip Lacovara declared, "We submit that this court should fully, explicitly, and decisively—and *definitively* —uphold Judge Sirica's decision."[12]

The justices met the next day to confer. All agreed that the concept of executive privilege was a valid one. But they also agreed that the Court's need for Nixon's tapes outweighed that privilege in this instance. The vote was unanimous. Nixon would have to turn over the tapes. But what form would their opinion take?

The Supreme Court can issue its decision in a variety of ways. Often a justice will agree with a majority decision, but not with the reasons behind it. Then he may attach a concurring opinion. A justice opposing a decision may write a dissent. Concurrences and dissents do not affect the outcome of a case. Those involved must obey the orders of the majority of voting justices. Attached opinions may influence future judges in deciding similar cases, though.

Brennan urged his fellow justices to issue one opinion, signed by all. This would emphasize complete agreement on the Court. Brennan was afraid that otherwise the president would ignore the Court's authority. Even Nixon must admit a unanimous vote would be a "definitive" opinion.

The justices still had to settle their differences. For the next two weeks, the justices wrote memos and talked with one another. Burger had assigned himself to write the opinion. As he drafted different versions, the other justices suggested changes, additions, and compromises.

Meanwhile, the press reported that the Supreme Court would not release its opinion soon. The newspapers said the Court was waiting for the House Judiciary Committee to vote on impeachment first. That way, the Court wouldn't influence the committee's decision.

This wasn't true, but it did mirror real concerns of the justices. Once the committee members knew that new evidence would be available, they might delay the vote. It could take months for transcripts to be available.

Finally the justices agreed they could not put off the decision on political grounds. Cases must be decided on their own merits. The justices continued to bicker over minor points. Finally Brennan appealed to them to compromise. If Nixon refused to comply, the Supreme Court's decisions would never again carry much weight. They needed to present a united front. The justices agreed.

On July 24, the Court reconvened. Nixon, it ruled, would have to release the tapes. When Jaworski saw that Burger, once a Nixon ally, was reading the opinion, he realized that the decision must have been unanimous. The justices stressed that their decision in the *Nixon v. Sirica* case applied only to the situation at hand. Future presidents could be secure in keeping their deliberations secret.

Chief of Staff Alexander Haig informed the president of the decision at Nixon's home in California. "I am gratified to note that the Court reaffirmed both the validity and the importance of the principle of executive privilege, the principle I had sought to maintain,"[13] Nixon announced later that day.

He sang a different tune to one of his lawyers, J. Fred Buzhardt. "There might be a problem with the June 23 tape, Fred,"[14] he told him.

Nixon had been reviewing his tapes. His conversation with Haldeman on June 23, 1972, was on one of the subpoenaed tapes. On the tape, Nixon and Haldeman schemed to have the CIA stop the FBI investigation of the Watergate break-in. It was the clearest evidence of obstruction of justice in any of the tapes.

"Well, we've found the smoking pistol,"[15] Buzhardt informed Haig after listening to the tape. Once the tape was turned over, there would be no way to hide Nixon's part in the conspiracy.

Over the next week, the House Judiciary Committee voted to recommend impeachment of the president. The committee charged Nixon with three specific offenses. The first article of impeachment was for obstructing justice. This was based on the hush money paid to the burglars and Nixon's orders to "stonewall it." The second charge was abuse of power. This stemmed from the use of government agencies to harass his "enemies." The third article of impeachment was for Nixon's defiance in ignoring the subpoenas of the House Judiciary Committee.

Meanwhile, the White House began releasing the tapes to Judge Sirica. On August 5, Nixon released a transcript of the June 23 tape to the public. The effect of the "smoking pistol" tape was devastating. What little support Nixon had left disappeared. It was clear that the full House membership would follow the Judiciary Committee's recommendation. Impeachment and probably conviction were inevitable.

Nixon did not want to be dragged through an ugly trial. He thought it would be best for the country if he stepped aside. On August 8, the president told the waiting nation, "I shall resign the presidency effective at noon tomorrow."[16]

Watergate Special Prosecutor Leon Jaworski waves as he speaks with reporters after the Supreme Court ruled President Richard Nixon must surrender White House tapes and papers sought by Jaworski.

CHAPTER EIGHT

Aftermath

*My God, what the hell have we done to
be impeached?*[1]

—**Richard Nixon to H. R. Haldeman**
April 20, 1973

Vice President Gerald Ford was sworn in as president
at noon by Chief Justice Burger on August 9, 1974. The country seemed glad to
have a leader who was free of the taint of Watergate. The feeling didn't last long.

On September 8, Ford called a press conference in the Oval Office. He
announced "a full, free, and absolute pardon unto Richard Nixon for all
offenses against the United States which he, Richard Nixon, has committed or
may have committed or taken part in during the period from January 20, 1969,
through August 9, 1974."[2]

Ford said he wanted to spare the country the undignified spectacle of
putting a former president on trial. He believed Nixon would never get a fair trial
and had suffered enough. The public didn't agree.

Telegrams flooded the White House condemning the pardon. The press
accused the new president of making a deal with Nixon. They suggested Nixon
had agreed to resign and turn over the presidency to Ford for a promise of a
pardon. Actually, Nixon had little to do with the selection of his second vice

**President Richard Nixon, accompanied by his wife, Pat, boards a plane as they leave
Andrews Air Force Base near Washington, D.C.**

president. Republican party leaders had suggested Ford. After Spiro Agnew's scandalous resignation, a noncontroversial figure like Ford was deemed best.

Nonetheless, Ford's popularity plummeted after the pardon. Voters had their revenge at the ballot box. Congressional elections that fall yielded a loss of 3 seats in the Senate and 43 seats in the House for the Republicans. Two years later, the pardon still haunted Ford. Nominated for reelection as president, he lost to Jimmy Carter. Carter was a relative unknown who campaigned on a "morality in government" platform.

Life went on for the principals in the Watergate scandal. Nixon retired to California, then New York. He has published several books, including an autobiography. As the stigma of his resignation faded, he emerged from seclusion. Subsequent administrations have occasionally looked to Nixon for advice, chiefly in the foreign affairs sphere.

Haldeman, Ehrlichman, and Mitchell all served prison terms of more than a year for their parts in the cover-up. Dean, Liddy, Colson, Magruder, Hunt, and McCord all served minor jail sentences as well. Many of the Watergate figures wrote books about their experiences. Those of Dean and Liddy became best-sellers.

Nixon's tapes have assumed an importance in legal history quite apart from their role in Nixon's downfall. Upon leaving office, Nixon made a deal with Ford to have his presidential records sent to his home in California. The agreement called for the tapes to be preserved for five years in case any were needed for evidence. After that time, Nixon could destroy any he wished. All the tapes were to be destroyed at Nixon's death.

Congress was outraged. In December 1974, the Presidential Recordings and Materials Preservation Act was passed. The act transferred control of the records from Nixon to the National Archives. Nixon filed suit to regain possession of the tapes and documents.

Every president, from George Washington on, had kept the records made during his term. In modern times, these records have ended up in presidential libraries. They provide the public with a historical account of the presidents' administrations.

Congress was afraid that Nixon wanted to distort the history of his sordid escapades. The courts agreed, saying Congress had "an adequate basis for concluding that Mr. Nixon might not be a wholly reliable custodian of the materials."[3]

Nixon objected to the Preservation Act on several grounds. He claimed that it violated his right to privacy. He said the act constituted illegal search and seizure, prohibited by the Fourth Amendment. Most importantly, he claimed executive privilege to keep the materials secret.

In 1977, the Supreme Court ruled against Nixon. The Court again restricted its opinion to Nixon's specific case. Nonetheless, the decision put further limits on presidential powers.

Through the years, Nixon, who died April 22, 1994, filed a variety of lawsuits to block public release of the tapes. The National Archives' staff has reviewed and edited more than 4,000 hours of tapes to remove private and confidential discussions. Twelve hours of the original tapes used in the Watergate trials have been available since 1980. The public can hear them at the National Archives annex in Alexandria, Virginia. The rest still await release.

Someday Nixon's secret tapes will lose their veil of mystery. That day will mark the end of an era. The power of American presidents has diminished since Nixon's smoking gun shattered his stone wall. But the power of truth and openness in government has grown. "It is time to open the door and let the public . . . see the documents and hear the tapes," a repentant John Ehrlichman recently wrote. "It is time to let the professional historians set out the events of the Nixon era with a clear, unbiased perspective that should be possible now."[4]

Source Notes

Introduction

1. Stanley I. Kutler, *The Wars of Watergate: The Last Crisis of Richard Nixon* (New York: Alfred A. Knopf, 1990), p. 618.

2. Bob Woodward and Carl Bernstein, *The Final Days* (New York: Avon Books, 1976), p. 503.

3. Kutler, p. 618.

Chapter One

1. *The Presidential Transcripts* (New York: Dell Publishing Co., 1974), p. 63.

2. Kutler, p. 190.

3. Ibid., p. 107.

4. Ibid., p. 199.

Chapter Two

1. Pamela Kilian, *What Was Watergate?* (New York: St. Martin's Press, 1990), p. 26.

2. Kutler, p. 190.

3. Ibid., p. 191.

4. Kilian, p. 24.

5. Arthur S. Link, Robert V. Remini, Douglas Greenberg, and Robert C. McMath, Jr., *A Concise History of the American People* (Arlington Heights, Ill.: Harlan Davidson, Inc., 1984), p. 541.

6. Woodward and Bernstein, p. 293.

7. Kilian, p. 26.

8. Ibid., p. 34.

9. Kutler, p. 254.

10. Ibid., p. 268.

11. Kilian, p. 40.

Chapter Three

1. Woodward and Bernstein, p. 126.

2. Kutler, p. 260.

3. *Presidential Transcripts*, p. 99.

4. Ibid.

5. Ibid., p. 110.

6. Ibid., p. 133.

7. Ibid.

8. Kutler, p. 261.

9. *Presidential Transcripts*, p. 30.

10. Kutler, p. 314.

11. *Presidential Transcripts*, p. 687.

12. Harold W. Chase and Craig R. Ducat, *Constitutional Interpretation: Cases—Essays—Materials* (St. Paul, Minn.: West Publishing Co., 1974), p. 315.

13. Ibid., p. 316.

14. Kilian, pp. 61-62.

15. Woodward and Bernstein, p. 511.

16. *Encyclopedia Americana*, International ed., 1993, s.v. "Nixon, Richard Milhous," p. 391.

Chapter Four

1. Chase and Ducat, p. 260.

2. Ibid.

3. Ibid., p. 262.

4. Ibid.

5. Ibid.

6. Ibid., p. 261.

7. Kilian, p. 70.

8. Chase and Ducat, p. 330.

9. Ibid., p. 265.

10. Kutler, p. 389.

11. Kilian, p. 72.

12. Kutler, p. 389.

13. Ibid.

Chapter Five

1. Woodward and Bernstein, p. 688.

2. Kilian, p. 76.

3. Kutler, p. 406.

4. Ibid., p. 414.

5. Kutler, p. 410.

6. Kilian, p. 78.

7. Ibid.

8. Ibid., p. 84.

9. *Presidential Transcripts*, p. xviii.

Chapter Six

1. Kutler, p. 508.

2. Bob Woodward and Scott Armstrong, *The Brethren: Inside the Supreme Court* (New York: Simon and Schuster, 1979), p. 287.

3. Ibid.

4. Chase and Ducat, p. 321.

5. Ibid.

6. Ibid., p. 279.

7. Link et al., p. A-5.

8. Chase and Ducat, p. 280.

9. Ibid.

10. Ibid., p. 298.

11. Ibid., p. 327.

12. Kutler, p. 123.

13. Ibid., p. 124.

14. Ibid., p. 125.

15. Link et al., p. A-8.

16. Chase and Ducat, p. 323.

17. Ibid., p. 325.

Chapter Seven

1. Kutler, p. 516.

2. *Presidential Transcripts*, p. 132.

3. Woodward and Armstrong, p. 298.

4. Ibid., p. 300.

5. Ibid., p. 303.

6. Ibid.

7. Ibid., p. 305.

8. Ibid., p. 306.

9. Ibid., p. 307.

10. Ibid.

11. Ibid., p. 308.

12. Ibid.

13. Kutler, p. 516.

14. Woodward and Bernstein, p. 285.

15. Ibid., p. 296.

16. Kilian, p. 124.

Chapter Eight

1. Kutler, p. 315.

2. Kilian, p. 111.

3. Lesley Oelsner, "Law Giving Nixon's Tapes to U.S. Is Upheld by Court," *New York Times*, Jan. 8, 1976, p. 1.

4. Seymour M. Hersh, "Nixon's Last Cover-up," *The New Yorker*, Dec. 14, 1992, p. 88.

Further Reading

Bernstein, Carl, and Bob Woodward. *All the President's Men*. New York: Simon and Schuster, 1974.

Cook, Fred J. *The Crimes of Watergate*. New York: Franklin Watts, 1981.

Coy, Harold. *The Supreme Court*, revised by Lorna Greenberg. New York: Franklin Watts, 1981.

Dash, Samuel. *Chief Counsel: Inside the Ervin Committee—the Untold Story of Watergate*. New York: Random House, 1976.

Dean, John W. *Blind Ambition: The White House Years*. New York: Simon and Schuster, 1976.

Ehrlichman, John. *Witness to Power: The Nixon Years*. New York: Simon and Schuster, 1982.

Ervin, Sam, Jr. *The Whole Truth: The Watergate Conspiracy*. New York: Random House, 1980.

Forte, David F. *The Supreme Court*. New York: Franklin Watts, 1979.

Goode, Stephen. *The Controversial Court: Supreme Court Influences on American Life*. New York: Julian Messner, 1982.

Greene, Carol. *The Supreme Court*. Chicago: Childrens Press, 1985.

Haldeman, H. R., with Joseph DiMona. *The Ends of Power*. New York: Times Books, 1978.

Hargrove, Jim. *Richard M. Nixon: The Thirty-seventh President*. Chicago: Childrens Press, 1985.

———. *The Story of Watergate*. Chicago: Childrens Press, 1988.

Jaworski, Leon. *The Right and the Power: The Prosecution of Watergate*. New York: Reader's Digest Press, 1976.

Kilian, Pamela. *What Was Watergate?* New York: St. Martin's Press, 1990.

McCord, James W., Jr. *A Piece of Tape; The Watergate Story: Fact and Fiction*. Rockville, Md.: Washington Media Services, 1974.

McKown, Robin. *The Resignation of Nixon: A Discredited President Gives Up the Nation's Highest Office*. New York: Franklin Watts, 1975.

Magruder, Jeb Stuart. *An American Life: One Man's Road to Watergate*. New York: Atheneum, 1974.

Mankiewicz, Frank. *U.S. vs. Richard M. Nixon: The Final Crisis*. New York: Quadrangle, 1975.

Marquardt, Dorothy A. *A Guide to the Supreme Court*. Indianapolis: Bobbs-Merrill, 1977.

New York Times. *The End of a Presidency*. New York: Bantam Books, 1974.

New York Times, ed. *Watergate Hearings: Break-in and Cover-up*. New York: Bantam Books, 1973.

Olds, Helen. *Richard Nixon*. New York: Putnam, 1970.

Peterson, Helen Stone. *The Supreme Court in America's Story*. Scarsdale, N.Y.: Garrard Publishing Co., 1976.

Pious, Richard M. *Richard M. Nixon*. Englewood Cliffs, N.J.: Julian Messner, 1991.

Sirica, John J. *To Set the Record Straight: The Break-in, the Tapes, the Conspirators, the Pardon*. New York: W. W. Norton, 1979.

Sussman, Barry. *The Great Cover-up: Nixon and the Scandal of Watergate*. New York: New American Library, 1974.

The Presidential Transcripts. New York: Dell, 1974.

Woodward, Bob, and Scott Armstrong. *The Brethren: Inside the Supreme Court*. New York: Avon Books, 1981.

Woodward, Bob, and Carl Bernstein. *The Final Days*. New York: Avon Books, 1976.

Index

Agnew, Vice President Spiro 46, *46*, 86

Baker, Senator Howard *31*, 37

Barker, Bernard 12, *15*, 21, 34

Bernstein, Carl 21

Blackmun, Justice Harry 60, 63, *74*

Brennan, Justice William 60, 62, *74*, 76, 78, 80, 81

Burger, Justice Warren 59, 60, 62, 63, *74*, 80, 81, 85

Butterfield, Alexander 37

Carter, President Jimmy 86

Central Intelligence Agency (CIA) 11, 14, 16, 20, 36, 69, 81

certiorari 60

Colson, Charles 14, 30, 54, 86

Committee for Nuclear Responsibility, Inc. v. Seaborg 70

Committee to Reelect the President (CRP) 14, 17, 18, 19, 20, 21, 23, 24, 34

Cox, Archibald 33, 38, 42, 44, 45, 47, *48*, 49, 50, 51, 52, 57, 77

Dean, John 11, 14, 20, 25, 26, 27, 30, 32, 33, 34, *35*, 36, 37, 43, 52, 53, 59, 75, 86

Douglas, Justice William O. 60, 62, *74*, 77, 78

Drinan, Representative Robert 38

Ehrlichman, John 32, 33, 34, 36, 37, 54, 62, 86, 87

Ellsberg, Daniel 16, 17, 32

Environmental Protection Agency v. Mink 67

Ervin, Senator Sam, Jr. 30, *31*, 34, 39, 42, 43

Federal Bureau of Investigation (FBI) 12, 14, 19, 20, 21, 25, *25*, 36, 50, 81

Fielding, Lewis 16, 17, 32, 34, 36

Ford, President Gerald 85, 86

Gemstone 18, 36

Gonzalez, Virgilio 12, *15*

Gray, Patrick L. 20, 25, *25*, 36, 37

Haig, Alexander 52, 81

Haldeman, H. R. 18, 19, 20, 21, 29, 32, 33, 34, 37, 52, 54, 75, 81, 85, 86

Hoover, J. Edgar 19

House Judiciary Committee 40, 54, 57, 71, 77, 78, 80, 81, 82

Hunt, Howard E. 12, 14, 23, 29, 30, 36, 53, 86

Huston Plan 36

Internal Revenue Service (IRS) 17,
36, 46

Jaworski, Leon 51, 52, 53, 54, 56,
57, 60, *61*, 77, 81, *83*

Kilbourn v. Thompson 42

Kleindienst, Richard 14, 33, 62

Liddy, Gordon G. 12, 14, 17, 18, 21,
21, 23, 24, 32, 36, 86

Magruder, Jeb 14, 23, 30, 32, 34, 86

Marshall, Chief Justice John *64*, 65

Marshall, Justice Thurgood *58*, 59,
60, 63, *74*, 76, 78

Martinez, Eugenio 12, *15*

McCord, James W. 11, 12, 14, *22*,
24, 29, 30, 34, 86

McGovern, Senator George 23

Mitchell, John 14, 18, 20, 21, 29, 30,
32, 34, 36, 52, 54, 62, *68*, 69, 86

New York Times v. U.S 16

Nixon v. Sirica 45, 65, 67-69, 81

Nixon, President Richard *1, 8*, 9-11,
14-20, *22*, 23-27, 29, 30, 32-34,
36-40, 42-47, *45*, 49-52, *53*, 54, *55*,
56, 57, 59, 60, 62, 63, 65, 70-72,
75-78, *79*, 80-82, *83*, *84*, 85-87

O'Brien, Lawrence 11, 12, 19

Pentagon Papers 16

Powell, Justice Lewis, Jr. 60, 63,
74, 76, 78

Rehnquist, Justice William 60, 62, *74*

Richardson, Elliot 33, 49, 50

Ruckelshaus, William 50

Saturday Night Massacre 50, 51

Senate Select Committee on Presidential Campaign Activities
(Senate Watergate Committee)
24, 30, *31*, *35*, 54

Sirica, Judge John 23, 24, *28*, 29,
30, 33, 38, 42, 44, 45, 51, 52, 53,
54, 57, 77, 80, 82

St. Clair, James 78, 79, 80

Stewart, Justice Potter 59, 60,
62, 63, *74*, 76

Sturgis, Frank 12, *15*

U.S. v. Reynolds 43, 70

U.S. v. The Washington Post 16

United States v. Burr 65

*United States v. United States Court
for the Eastern District of
Michigan* 69

Walters, Vernon 20

White, Justice Byron 60, 63, *74*, 76

Woods, Rose Mary 52, *53*

Woodward, Bob 21

Wright, Charles Alan 42, 43, *43*, 44,
45, 51, 70

*Youngstown Sheet & Tube Co. v.
Sawyer* 66